JOHN FOSTER
The Land of the Flibbertigibbets

JOHN FOSTER is the well-known anthologist of over 150
collections of poetry for children, including the best-
selling *Twinkle Twinkle Chocolate Bar*. He is the author
of twelve books of his own poetry for children, such as
Four O'Clock Friday and *The Poetry Chest* — a collection
of over 250 of his original poems, and of two rhyming
dictionaries — the *Oxford First Rhyming Dictionary* and
the *Oxford Junior Rhyming Dictionary*.

Also by John Foster

SOLO COLLECTIONS FOR CHILDREN
Four O'Clock Friday (Oxford University Press 1991)
Standing on the Sidelines (Oxford University 1995)
You Little Monkey (Oxford University Press 1996, 2002)
Word Wizard (Oxford University Press 2001)
The Poetry Chest (Oxford University Press 2007)

ANTHOLOGIES FOR CHILDREN
Twinkle Twinkle Chocolate Bar (Oxford University Press 1991, 2009)
Dinosaur Poems ill. Korky Paul (Oxford University Press 1993, 2004)
My First Oxford Book of Poems (Oxford University Press 2000, 2006)
My First Oxford Book of Christmas Poems (Oxford University Press 200, 2007)
The Works 8 (Macmillan 2009)

RHYMING DICTIONARIES
Oxford First Rhyming Dictionary (Oxford University Press 2003, 2008)
Oxford Junior Rhyming Dictionary (Oxford University Press 2005, 2008)

JOHN FOSTER

The Land of
the Flibbertigibbets

❖

CHILDREN'S POETRY LIBRARY
No. 10

SALT

LONDON

PUBLISHED BY SALT PUBLISHING
Dutch House, 307–308 High Holborn,
London WC1V 7LL United Kingdom

First published 2011

Printed in Great Britain by the MPG Books Group,
Bodmin and King's Lynn

Typeset in Oneleigh 11 / 14

ISBN 978 1 84471 288 5 paperback

1 3 5 7 9 8 6 4 2

for Chris

CONTENTS

ACKNOWLEDGEMENTS

Some of the poems included in this book were first published in other collections as follows:

'In the Land of the Flibbertigibbets' from *The Poetry Chest* by John Foster (OUP); 'The Spotted Origami' from *Four O'Clock Friday* by John Foster (OUP); 'This is a Troll Bridge', 'Anna's All Star Band', 'Threats', 'In My Mind's Eye', 'Behind the Raised Eyebrow', and 'Inside a Shell' from *The Works 8* compiled by John Foster (Macmillan); 'Beware the Draculasaurus', and 'Di Knows What's Best for Dinosaurs' from *Dinosaur Poems* compiled by Paul Cookson (Scholastic); 'The Name of the Game' from *The World at Our Feet* compiled by Paul Cookson (Macmillan); 'Spells' from *Standing on the Sidelines* by John Foster (OUP); 'The Grand Old Count of York' from *The Jumble Book* compiled by Roger Stevens (Macmillan).

I AM A POEM

I am a poem.
Read me and dream.

I am a poem.
Recite me and sing.

I am a poem.
Perform me and dance.

I am a poem.
Listen to my magic music.

IN THE LAND OF THE FLIBBERTIGIBBETS

In the land of the Flibbertigibbets,
The Curlybirds whirl and whiz,
The Googlies giggle, the Rampoons wriggle
And the Furzles flitter and fizz,
    The Furzles flitter and fizz.

In the land of the Flibbertigibbets,
The Humdrums simper and sing,
The Bamboozles bump, the Jamborees jump
And the Plimpets zip and ping,
    The Plimpets zip and ping.

In the land of the Flibbertigibbets,
The Dobblers dibble and dive,
The Clutters clatter, the Chitters chatter,
And the Junkets jiggle and jive,
    The Junkets jiggle and jive.

IN LOOKING-GLASS LAND

In Looking-Glass Land
I always see
Another child who looks like me.

But if I ask her out to play,
She sadly smiles,
As if to say:

'There's nothing more I'd like to do
Than step outside
And play with you.

But not today.'
And then she turns her head away,
Because she knows
That she must stay

Inside the glass
That is her home
And never never ever roam.

In Looking-Glass Land
I always see
A child inside who looks like me.

THE WIZARD'S DRAGON

I am the wizard's dragon.
I speak with tongues of flame.
I am the wizard's dragon.
Firesnorter is my name.

I guard the room where he keeps
His secret book of spells.
I guard the dungeons where he keeps
His demons in their cells.

Day and night I keep watch
As I patrol the skies,
Searching out intruders
With my penetrating eyes.

Scattered round the castle's grounds
Are the bones of those who've died,
Scorched to death by my fiery breath
As they tried to get inside.

I am the wizard's dragon.
I speak with tongues of flame.
I am the wizard's dragon.
Firesnorter is my name.

THE SPOTTED ORIGAMI

The Spotted Origami
Is missing from its cage.
We think it could be hiding here —
Somewhere on this page.

Its tiny eyes — about the size
Of pinheads — are jet black.
Its feet are shaped like question marks
And leave an inky track.

It's paper-thin with snow-white skin.
Its spots are snow-white too.
If you should catch a glimpse of it,
Please telephone the zoo.

THIS IS A TROLL-BRIDGE

This is a troll-bridge.
Cross it if you dare.
This is a troll-bridge.
Beware! Beware!

The trolls are waiting,
Lurking in their lair.
This is a troll-bridge.
Please take care!

THE GRAND OLD COUNT OF YORK

The Grand Old Count of York
He had ten thousand bats.
He kept them in his wardrobe
Hanging from his cloaks and hats.
And when he went out they flew out.
And when he went in they flew in.
And when they were neither in nor out
They haunted his neighbours' flats

WHEN DRACULA WENT TO THE DOCTOR

When Dracula went to the doctor,
The doctor said with a sigh,
'It's your usual problem, sir,
Your blood count is very high.'

BEWARE THE DRACULASAURUS

Beware the Draculasaurus
Who roams graveyards at night.
Don't let him grab you by the throat.
He's thirsty for a bite!

The other dinosaurs are dead.
Their bones have turned to stone.
Only Draculasaurus lives —
A monster all alone.

His bloodshot eyes glow in the dark
His fingernails are claws.
Beware his razor teeth.
Beware his slavering jaws.

As he lurks behind the tombstones,
The moon glints on each scale.
He's waiting there to wrap you up
In his forked serpent's tail.

Beware the Draculasaurus
Who roams graveyards at night.
Don't let him grab you by the throat.
He's thirsty for a bite!

DI KNOWS WHAT'S BEST FOR DINOSAURS

Di knows what's best for dinosaurs.
For glistening scales and sharpened claws,
Visit *Di's 4 Dinosaurs.*

Whether you're two tonnes or ten tonnes,
Let our giant crane take the strain
And hoist you into our lake
For a refreshing dip.

Then visit our shower hall
For a steam-clean and a power-scrub
Before enjoying a scale-polishing session
In our polishing parlour.

Sharpen up your claws and spikes
On our knife-grinding machines,
Or practise your tail-whipping
In our fully-equipped gym.

Smarten up your snarl
With a full facial
That will leave you looking grim and gruesome.

And have a snack in our gourmet café.
Our specialities include
Spiced shrubs for vegetarians
And mammoth pie for the meat-eater.

Di knows what's best for dinosaurs.
For glistening scales and sharpened claws
Visit *Di's 4 Dinosaurs*.

A dinosaur whatever their size
Will never forget a visit to Di's!

A CHEEKY BOY CALLED ROBERT RUNG

A cheeky boy called Robert Rung
Was always sticking out his tongue
At everybody that he saw
Passing by the village store.
Till one day he went too far.
A driver, leaping from his car,
Shouted out, 'You little toad!'
And chased Robert down the road
Into a farmyard nearby,
Where Robert slipped and, with a cry,
Fell headlong in a steaming pile
Of manure, squelchy and vile,
So that cheeky Robert Rung
Was covered, head to foot in dung.
Which is why when you are young
You never should stick out your tongue.

YOU'RE FOR THE HIGH JUMP!

'You're for the high jump!'
Said my dad
When he caught me
Jumping up and down on the sofa.

What does he mean?
That he's going to buy the trampoline
I've always wanted
Or that he's planning
To play leapfrog with me
In the back garden.

By the look on his face,
I'd better not
Jump to any conclusions.

MY BROTHER'S ALLERGIES

When my brother had to go into hospital
They asked my mum
If he had any allergies.
'Yes,' she said,
'Lots. He's allergic to
      Getting up in the morning,
      Tidying his room,
      Doing the washing up, and
      Listening to what I say.
What's more,' she added,
'According to his teacher,
He's allergic to homework.'

GRANDPA'S FALSE TEETH

When Grandpa's false teeth fell on the floor,
Before he could catch them they ran through the door.

They ran down the steps and into the street,
Where they started to gnaw at a passer-by's feet.

When Grandpa came running and begged them to stop,
They snapped at his heels and ran into a shop.

When the shopkeeper said, 'You can't come in here.
No teeth are allowed!' They just gave a sneer.

They jumped on a shelf full of sweets in their jars
And started to nibble at two chocolate bars.

The shopkeeper gave a despairing groan
And pressed 9 9 9 on his mobile phone.

The teeth burst out laughing, 'You'll never catch us!'
Ran out of the shop and jumped onto a bus.

They said to the driver, 'Two singles to Ware.'
And, as far as I know, they're still living there.

While Grandpa sits toothless, twiddling his thumbs,
Stroking his chin and sucking his gums!

IN MEMORY OF BILLY GREEN

In memory of Billy Green
Who took off in a time-machine.
To see the future was his aim,
But he discovered that the claim
It would go forwards wasn't true.
Instead, it flew off backwards to
Prehistoric times where he saw
The footprints of a dinosaur.
But Billy Green was out of luck.
To his dismay the joystick stuck.
He heard a roar and then he saw
Tyrannosaurus raise a claw
With which he smashed to smithereens
Poor Billy and his time-machine.
And so the future was not seen
By the luckless Billy Green
Who travelled to the past instead
And found that dinosaurs weren't dead.

EPITAPHS

HERE LIES A ROBOT

Here lies a robot.
Deprived of grease,
He ceased to work.
May he rust in peace.

PETER TIMES, HISTORIAN

In better times, Peter Times
Passed his time studying past times.
But the past caught up with him
And now he's passed away.

BETTY BROOM

Here lies a cleaner, Betty Broom,
Now she sweeps inside this tomb.

MISS CHATTERBOX

Here lies Miss Chatterbox,
Who chattered and chattered all day.
She chattered and chattered and chattered,
Till she chattered herself away.

THE NAME OF THE GAME

My first is in ref and twice in offside.
My second's in throw-in and twice in boot.
My third is in scored, but not in saved
My fourth is in penalty and in shoot.
My fifth's twice in dribble, but not in kick.
My sixth is in transfer, but not in fee.
My seventh is in league, but not in premier.
My eighth is in goal — To play you need me!

HOW TO MAKE A FOOTBALL

The Word Wizard said:
Take an *o*.
Add a t and indicate
the direction you are travelling *to*.
Stick another o on the end
and you'll find also there *too*.
Drop in an f, give the letters a stir
and you've got one to stand on — *foot*.

Now make a ball.
Start at the beginning with an *a*.
Place a b in front of it
and award yourself a university degree — *B.A.*
Throw in an l and juggle the letters
To make a place where you can experiment — *lab*.
Put an l in front,
then read the letters backwards
and you've made a bouncy one — *ball*.

Next, put your foot against it
And give it a good kick — *football*.

BEST SELLING FOOTBALL BOOKS

Only the Goalie to Beat	by Willie Score
Understanding the Offside Trap	by Izzie Onside
It's a Knockout	by F.A.Cup
Appealing to the Ref	by R.U. Serious
Losing Possession	by Miss Kick
Sent Off	by Earl E. Bath
Football Hooligans Named and Shamed	by U.R.Stupid
Tales from the Lower Leagues	by Carl Isle and Don Caster
How I Scored the Goal That Won the Cup	by U.Wish
The Final Whistle	by I. Blewit

FOOTBALL HAIKU

GOAL!

From a corner kick,
The striker rises, heads the ball
Into the net. Goal!

PENALTY

The full-back lunges.
The striker falls. The ref blows
And points to the spot.

SENT OFF

Tackled from behind,
The striker retaliates
And gets a red card.

OFFSIDE

The striker races through.
But he's made his move too soon.
The flag waves: Offside.

MISSED

Only six yards out,
An open goal. The striker
Slips, slices the ball wide.

THERE WAS AN OLD WOMAN

There was an old woman who lived in a boot.
She taught all her children to know how to shoot.
She taught them to keep their heads over the ball,
While bending it over a defensive wall.
She taught them to tackle and how to defend
Before selling them all to Preston North End.

MARY'S DAD WAS FOOTBALL MAD

Mary's dad was football mad.
While she was still in her pram,
He dressed her up in a football strip
And taught her to say Tottenham.

FINAL SCORES

Wanderers 1   Stay-at-homes 0
United 6   Divided 0
Villa 1   Mansion 2
Pompey 1   Caesar 1
Saints 2   Sinners 2
Wednesday 1   Thursday 2
Forest 3   Shrubbery 0
Hammers 0   Screwdrivers 1
Rangers 2   Poachers 1
Gunners 4   Archers 0

LET'S GIVE A CHEER FOR ONOMATOPEIA

Are you ready? Are you ready?
Start the fizzing and the whizzing
Start the rapping and the clapping
Start the humming and the drumming
Start the snipping and the snapping
Let's give a welcome cheer
For onomatopoeia!

With a pitter-pat-a-pat
And a rattling rat-a-tat
With a splutter and a splatter
With a chitter and a chatter
With a clinking and a clunking
With a plinking and a plunking
With a hee-haw and a boo-hoo
With an oompah and a yoo-hoo
Join in and give a cheer
For onomatopoeia!

With a grunting and a growling
With a yowling and a howling
With a squealing and a squeaking
With a squawking and a shrieking
With a jibber and a jabber
With a ting-a-ling-a-ling
With a tooting and a hooting
With a ring-a-ding-ding
Let's hear it loud and clear
Let's give a final cheer
For onomatopoeia!

HAVE YOU HEARD?

The *splink* of water as it drips from a tap
The *slithing* of waves as they gently lap
The *phurring* of the air from a hairdryer
The *wrackle* of wood as it burns in the fire
The *gliss* of skates as they glide over ice
The *crittering* scutter of scratching mice
The *glud* of a boxer punching with his fist
The *gloan* of the crowd as a penalty's missed
The *shloosh* of melting snow dropping off trees
The *swuttering* of leaves blowing in the breeze
The *phwerp* of air from a deflating balloon
The *trinkle* as you tap a glass with a spoon
The *treeking* of a startled bird
The *plur* of a gently whispered word

WHAT DO YOU CALL...

What do you call

an angry father	a mad dad
a stupid idler	a lazy crazy
a stinking boot	a smelly wellie
a classroom joker	a school fool
a gleaming car	a clean machine
a thin girl	a skinny Minnie
an odd rabbit	a funny bunny
an escaped elk	a loose moose
a tardy friend	a late mate
a nightmare	a scream-dream

ANAGRAM ANTICS

Waddle about and drag your feet.
Twist around *skate* for meat to eat.

Mix up *races* to give someone a fright.
Make *stone* into messages you write.

Wipe away *tears* and then give me a look.
Turn *votes* into something on which to cook.

Untie *loop* to find a place to dive in.
Knead *bread* into hairs that grow on a chin.

Stir up *late* into a story to tell.
Shuffle *leap* into the sound of a bell.

Spin *reaps* into a weapon to throw.
Juggle *times* to strike with a heavy blow.

BACKWARDS AND FORWARDS

Why are buns like a snub?
Why is a reed like a deer?
Why is a keel like a leek?
Why is a reel like a leer?

Why is peels like sleep?
Why is loops like a spool?
Why is doom like mood?
And why is loot like a tool?

GEOGRAPHICAL DEFINITIONS

A reef is a knot of coral.
A down is a soft coat of hair growing on a grassy upland.
A peak is a glimpse of a mountain summit.
A plateau is a high level of flattery.
A geyser is an old bloke spouting forth.
A gully is a cricketer fielding in a small valley.
A headwind is a polite term for a belch.
A meander is a boy and girl strolling along a river-bank.

TRAVELLERS' TALES

In Mexico
There's a TV show
Hosted by a buffalo.

In Hong Kong
When they bang a gong
Everyone bursts into song.

In Japan
People who can
Can-can.

In Nicaragua
You'll often see a jaguar
Strumming a guitar in a bar.

In Rome
People often stay at home
Playing cards with their garden gnome.

In Rangoon
Every afternoon
A baboon plays tunes on a bassoon.

In Singapore
There's an annual tug-of-war
With a dinosaur.

In Peru
You can practise kung-fu
With a kangaroo.

In Uruguay
Everyone's camera-shy —
I don't know why.

And, at Hallowee'n,
In Bethnal Green
You can see the Queen
Bouncing on a trampoline.

THE ITINERANT WORKER

I started work in Workington, but it didn't work out.
So I travelled the country seeking a suitable job.
I worked in a snack bar in Sandwich,
And in a laundry in Washington.
I worked as a plumber in Waterlooville
And as a dog-handler in Kenilworth.
I worked as a locksmith in Keighley
And as a florist in Bloomsbury.
I worked in a boot factory in Wellington
And as a refuse collector in Skipton.
I worked as a haulage contractor in Carterton
And as a tree surgeon in Poplar.
I worked as a ploughman in Harrow
And as a stableboy in Saddleworth.
Finally, I worked as an undertaker in Gravesend
And as a gravedigger in Bury.

I USED TO WORK

I used to work as a butcher but I got the chop.
I used to work as an electrician till I became switched off.
I used to work as a footballer but they kicked me out.
I used to work as a fisherman but the job was rather fishy.
I used to work as an optician but I couldn't see eye to eye
      with my colleagues.
I used to work as a bouncer but they threw me out.
I used to work as a pilot but I left under a cloud.
I used to work as a chef but I made a hash of it.
I used to work as a typist but I found I was the wrong type.
I used to work as a dishwasher before the work dried up.
I used to work as an undertaker until I got boxed in.

BY DEFINITION: SCENTS

Descent: The musty mystery of an underground vault.
Ascent: The fresh air at a mountain's summit.
Crescent: The soft aroma of the new moon.
Incandescent: The acrid reek of a raging inferno.
Adolescent: The sweaty stench of unwashed socks.
Putrescent: The stink of decaying vegetation.
Iridescent: The sweet fragrance of a smile.
Quiescent: The perfume of a kindly thought.

CLASSIFIED ANTS

pant

(i) an out-of-breath ant
(ii) an undercover ant
(iii) a musical ant that plays quietly

important

an ant brought in from another country

ascendant

an up-and-coming ant

flamboyant

a young male ant who likes showing off

flippant

a gymnastic ant

cant

an ant who keeps on repeating
meaningless statements

elegant

a fashionably-dressed ant

discordant

an ant that sings out-of-tune

pendant

(i) a hanger-on
(ii) an ant kept in captivity

ANIMAL COMPLAINTS

'I'm just a dogsbody,' complained the dog.
'What about me? I do the donkey work,' replied the donkey.
'Don't be such as ass,' interrupted the pig.
'I'm the one who has to give piggy-backs.'
'You're pigheaded,' squawked the hen.
'At least you're not henpecked.'
'Well I am,' retorted the horse.
'I'm not allowed to indulge in any horseplay.'
'And I have to take care not to slip on any cowslips,'
Moaned the cow.
'Every night someone insists on counting us,'
Bleated the sheep sheepishly.
'And I'm fed up of being a nanny,' the goat butted in.
Meanwhile, the bull dozed.

HOW TO MAKE A TEACHER

The word wizard said:
Start with a T.
Add an a
And don't forget to say thank you *Ta*
Mix in an r
And either find a rodent *Rat*
Or the sticky substance
That is used to make roads *Tar*.
Put in an e, but don't start crying,
It's just a homonym *Tear*,
Which can also be pronounced
To show that you want to rip things apart.
Now find a c, stir thoroughly
And find a wooden container *Crate*.
Drop in a second e
And you'll make something appear *Create*.
All you need to do now
Is to find an h, to put the letters in a spin
And you'll have made a *Teacher*.

THE WORD WIZARD SAID: GIVE YOURSELF A BREAK

Start with yourself:
I
Add the first letter of tag
And become the chaser:
It
Now take an e, shuffle and make a knot:
Tie
Insert an r and become weary:
Tire
Put in a p, stir and get some food
That is not to everyone's taste:
Tripe
Add an s and get one in line:
Stripe
Or a ghostly spirit
Sprite
Add another e, stir again
And get a break from these puzzles:
Respite.

ANNA'S ALL-STAR BAND

(a univolic)

Anna has a band—
Anna's band raps raps—
Madcap ragbag claptrap raps.

Sharks snap jaws
Jackals jam jazz
Crabs clap claws—
Razzmatazz.

Llamas chant psalms
Swans twang saws
Carps clasp harps
And cats tap paws.

Ants bang pans
Rats rat-a-tat
A calf cancans
And yaks yak-yak.

Anna has a band—
Anna's band raps raps—
Madcap ragbag claptrap raps.

Z'S A ZIPPER-ZAPPER

Z's a Zipper-Zapper.
He's a zebra who's a rapper.
Z is short for zero, Z is short for zone.
You can even text Z on your mobile phone.

Z's a Zigger-Zagger.
He's a Zulu with a swagger.

Z's the start of zealot.
He's the start of zest.
You can find him at the zenith.
Z will always do his best.

Z's a Zipper-Zapper.
He's a zebra who's a rapper.

Z can blow a zephyr
Through the branches of a tree.
In Greek Z stands for zeta.
In the US he's called zee.

Z's a Zigger-Zagger.
He's a Zulu with a swagger.

You'll find him twice in Zanzibar
And once in Mozambique.
In lazy and amazing
He's playing hide and seek.

Z's a Zipper-Zapper.
He's a zebra who's a rapper.

Z can play a zither.
Z can zing and zoom.
Z can push a zimmer
Around a living-room.

Z's a Zigger-Zagger.
He's a Zulu with a swagger.

Z can put a Z-bend on a mountain track.
Z can teach you all about the Zodiac.
Z is first in zombie and in zebu too,
In zabaglione, in zinc and zoo.

Z's the zaniest character you've ever met.
He's number 26 in the alphabet.

ADVERBIALLY SPEAKING

Murmuring softly, shouting loudly,
Asking anxiously, stating proudly.
Nattering noisily, chattering lazily,
Explaining clearly, muttering crazily.
Uttering quietly, whispering gently,
Chatting idly, gossiping intently.
Talking seriously, arguing furiously,
Requesting politely, enquiring curiously.

IT'S A QUESTION OF
HOMONYMS

Can you propose a toast to a slice of toast
Or send a wooden post through the post?
Can you put a patch on a vegetable patch
Or make a good match at a football match?
Can you skip school if you fall in a skip
Or be sure not to trip on a holiday trip?
Can you float a milk float down a river
Or make a quiver full of arrows quiver?
Can you sling a slingshot with your arm in a sling
Or use a mobile phone to ring a diamond ring?
Just give this poem another quick skim
To understand what it means to be a homonym.

EXCEPTIONAL PASTS

If the past tense of ring is rung,
Shouldn't the past tense of bring be brung?
If the past tense of swim's swum or swam,
Why isn't the past tense of skim skum or skam?
If the past tense of write is wrote,
Shouldn't the past tense of bite be bote?
If the past tense of drink's drank or drunk,
Why isn't the past tense of think thank or thunk?
If the past tense of hit is hit,
Shouldn't the past tense of sit be sit?
Surely this proves there's no sense
In how we form the past tense?

THINGS THAT SOUND OLD

A frozen pond with cold in it.
A treasure chest with gold in it.
A paper with a fold in it.
A phone call with a hold in it.
A brave deed with a bold in it.
A telling-off with scold in it.
A wonder with "Behold!" in it.
A storybook with told in it.

A long walk with a strolled in it.
A ballot-box with polled in it.
A muddy dog with rolled in it.
A cricket stump with bowled in it.
A tearstain with consoled in it.
A persuasion with cajoled in it.
A church bell with a tolled in it.
An auction with a SOLD in it.

BLOWING HOT AND COLD

If your problem is a hot potato,
Do you pass it on or eat it instead?
Do you keep yourself warm when it's freezing
Or hatch plots inside a hotbed?
Do you rub ointment on a cold shoulder
Or take offence at a slight?
Is out in the cold to be ignored
Or a walk on a winter's night?
Are you in hot water when taking a bath
Or does it spell trouble for you?
Do you get hot under the collar in sunshine
And filled with annoyance too?
Will pouring cold water put out a fire
Or pour scorn on an idea?
Do you get cold feet without any socks
Or from opting out due to fear?
Is hotfooting it toasting your toes
Or making a quick getaway?
Is a load of hot air idle chatter
Outside on a summer's day?

UNDERSTANDING UNCLE SAM

Can you skip down the sidewalk to the candy store?
Can you fall in the fall on the forest floor?
Can you say 'Sure thing' and drawl 'Doggone'?
Can you ask the way to the nearest john?
Can you take a raincheck on a movie trip?
Can you drive down the highway to Sunset Strip?
Can you open the trunk or the hood of a car?
Can you pick out a cookie from a cookie jar?
Can you fill up an auto with gasoline?
Can you make a date with the new prom queen?
Can you change a diaper or sling a slingshot?
Can you put up a billboard in a vacant lot?
Can you buy molasses at a five and dime?
Can you go to the ocean at holiday time?
If you can say 'You're welcome' and 'Howdy, ma'am'
You're on your way to understanding Uncle Sam.

HEY DIDDLE DIDDLE

Hey diddle diddle
Pig in the middle
A cow in a hot-air balloon,
A dog and a cat
And a rat in a hat
Went to tea with the Man in the Moon,

They had burgers galore
And chips by the score
And slices of cheese from the moon.
On the return trip
They all had a kip
While the dish danced a jig with the spoon.

BEDBUG, BEDBUG

Bedbug, bedbug,
Where have you been?
'I've been up to London
To visit the Queen.'

Bedbug, bedbug,
What did you do?
'I bit the Queen's bottom.
I bit the King's too!'

RIDDLE

My first is in first and also in second.
My second is in second but not in first.
My third is in second but not in third.
My fourth is in third and also in fourth.
My fifth is in second, but not third or fourth.
My sixth is in fourth, in fifth and in sixth.

My whole is hidden inside a box.
To find me just undo the locks.

SPELLS

I crackle and spit. I lick and leap higher.
This is the spell of the raging fire.

I clasp and grasp. I grip in a vice.
This is the spell of torturing ice.

I claw and scratch. I screech and wail.
This is the spell of the howling gale.

I clash and crash. I rip asunder.
This is the spell of booming thunder.

I whisper. I stroke. I tickle the trees.
This is the spell of the evening breeze.

I slither. I slide. I drift. I dream.
This is the spell of the murmuring stream.

THREATS

'Unless you let me through,' said the wind,
'I will batter all night at your door.
I will tear up your trees by the roots
And rip the slates from your roof.'

'Unless you treat me with respect,' said the fire,
'I will devour your forests with my flames.
I will set light to your homes
And reduce them to smouldering ruins.'

'Unless you watch your step,' said the ice,
'I will make you dance to my tune.
I will make you slither and slide
And fall flat on your face.'

AFTER THE STORM

(three haiku)

For twenty-four hours
The rain poured incessantly
Flooding fields and homes.

Once there was a bridge.
Now there is only a gap
Where the water rages.

The bankside pillars
Still stand as if a large tooth
Has been extracted.

TOOTHACHE IS A TORTURER

Toothache is a torturer,
Constantly throbbing away,
Sending jolts of agony
That keep you from sleeping,
Until you are driven,
Despite memories of drills and injections,
To confess that you are desperate
To go to the dentist.

SIX CLERIHEWS

EDMUND CLERIHEW BENTLEY

Edmund Clerihew Bentley
Said, 'I recently
Had nothing better to do,
So I invented the clerihew.'

ROMAN ABRAMOVICH

Roman Abramovich
Was so rich
He was able to fulfil his dream
Of making Chelsea a great football team.

MOHAMMED ALI

Mohammed Ali
Said, 'I stung like a bee.
When put to the test,
I was the greatest!'

JACQUES COUSTEAU

Jacques Cousteau
Said that down below
On the ocean floor
He saw creatures galore.

COCO THE CLOWN

Coco the clown
Never wore a frown
When he walked round town
And his trousers fell down.

LEWIS HAMILTON

Lewis Hamilton
Is a phenomenon.
His one-track mind
Leaves his rivals far behind.

TWO KENNINGS

BOOK

Page-turning
Tale-telling
Spellbinder.

Plot-hatching
Cliffhanging
Suspense-spinner.

Spine-shivering
Thrill-chilling
Mystery-twister.

Mind-bending
Surprise-ending
Story-weaver.

CAR

Motorway-speeding
Journey-taker
Gas-guzzling
Fume-maker.

Gear-changing
Overtaker
Tyre-squealing
Swift-braker

Slow-moving
Traffic-queuer
Non-stopping
Drive-througher.

Lorry-passing
Mover-and-shaker
Caravan-pulling
Take-a-breaker.

DIAMOND POEM

Snow —
Soft flakes
Dust the street,
Painting pavements
A   brilliant   white.
In the lamp's light,
Glittering
Crystals
Gleam.

I AM A FREE VERSE POEM

I am a free verse poem.
I am not shackled
by the constraints of form.
My words can wander across the page
without having to worry
about the number of syllables per line
or the need to rhyme.
If I feel like it,

                              up
            I can go   and
                      down,
sdrawkcab and forwards.
There are no boundaries confining me,
no set of rules that I must follow.
I am happier than a haiku.
The song I sing is my own.
I can pattern the page
however I like.
I am a free verse poem.

IN MY MIND'S EYE

I saw the caged bird
flying free in the sunlit sky.

I saw the pacing bear
loping across the Arctic ice.

I saw the hunted fox
nuzzling her cubs in her den.

I saw the bloodied seal
somersaulting in the waves.

I saw the refugee child
skipping across a village square.

I saw the homeless vagrant
digging in the garden of his home.

I saw the tortured prisoner
dancing in a carnival procession.

I saw the lifeless soldier
cradling his newborn son.

EPIGRAMS

ON CONSCIENTIOUS OBJECTORS

To hold to their beliefs is brave and strong.
To punish them for doing so is wrong.

ON PEOPLE OF DIFFERENT FAITHS

What they believe you may not think is true,
But they deserve as much respect as you.

ON A DICTATOR

Your human rights mean not a thing to him,
But opposition risks both life and limb.

ON DISPUTES

It's better to resolve disputes by law
Than violently to settle up the score.

BEHIND THE RAISED EYEBROW

Behind the raised eyebrow
I glimpsed a host of silent questions.
Behind the scornful grin
I heard the snigger of derision.
Behind the tearstained cheeks
I tasted the salt of wasted wishes.
Behind the odour of sweat
I smelt the scent of fear.
Behind the touch of a hand
I felt the faint stirrings of hope.

INSIDE A SHELL

Inside a shell
There is the whisper of a wave.
Inside a feather
There is the breath of a breeze.
Inside an ember
There is the memory of a flame.
Inside a rock
There is the murmur of a mountain.
Inside a well
There is the echo of a wish.
Inside a seed
There is the promise of a flower.